The Creatively Imagined Explanation of Gabriel's Blue Giraffe

Photo Illustrations by Kimiya & *Taljon Photography*
Additional art work by the Participants
Who have the Bravery, Courage & Freedom to color OuTsiDe the lines!

The Creatively Imagined Explanation of

Gabriel's Blue Giraffe

Printed in the United States of America.

For information contact:
Kingdom Enterprises International Publishing
P.O. Box 122181
Arlington, Texas 76012
www.KingdomEnterprisesInternational.com
www.DestinyCenter.com

Destiny Center is a division of Kingdom Enterprises International.

ISBN 978-1-62849-024-4

Cover design and all photo illustrations are by Kimiya & Taljon Photography.

In Honor of Sheeba

Peter & Sheeba,

The testimony of your Faith
Is the inspiration for this book.

You are both such a StRoNg source of
constant encouragement & faithful fellowship.

May the Lord bless the Family Legacy
you are continuing on in
as you both birth forth New Adventures with
your son Gabriel.

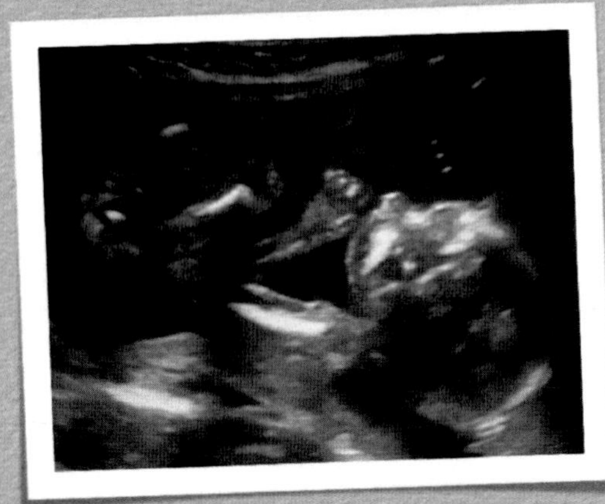

For Gabriel

Because we have long awaited
and excitedly looked forward
to your Joyous Arrival.

You are the SuBsTaNcE of
what we have HoPeD for
and you are the EVIDENCE of
what we KNEW was
CREATIVELY & imaginably
POSSIBLE with Jesus as our Lord!

m a y b e & p e r h a p s...

Two terms that are helpful in coming to terms with,
so we can Trust God better with the
unexpected uncertainties & possible disappointments
of life.
Finding and Giving ForGiveNess
within God's Perfect LoVe.

m a y b e & p e r h a p s...
Two terms that invite us into the
Adventurous Freedoms & Endless Fun of
Partnering with our Creator in
Creating & Imagining the Limitless PoSsiBiLiTiEs that
we have access to, when we put our Trust & Faith in God!

Biggest "G"

BiG "G" and Little "g"

The biggest "G" ever is for God,
because God is Good.
He loves us Greatly. He is Generous and
God is Gracious to us with His Grace.

Big "G" is for Gabriel who is Good .
Gabriel is a boy who Giggles and Grows and can imagine Great things ...because God made Gabriel that way.

Little "g" is for giraffe.
Giraffe's can be great fun
because God was being very creative when He made giraffes.

On This Page
Practice Writing G and g

why GOD is GOOD?

God is Good
because He gave us all Gabriel
to enjoy and love and giggle with
as we watch Gabriel grow and do great imaginable things.

God is also good
because He gave Gabriel a blue giraffe
to play with and
have fun with and
to be creative with and
to imagine stuff with.

Let's see if we can have fun and be creative while imagining stuff about Gabriel's blue giraffe that God gave to Gabriel!?!

Why is Gabriel's giraffe blue?

Gabriel's blue giraffe is not sad is he? Some people get blue when they feel sad.
But Gabriel's giraffe is not the kind of blue that is sad.
Gabriel's blue giraffe is happy and cuddly when he is with Gabriel.

maybe...

Maybe Gabriel's blue giraffe became blue because
he might'a could'a fell into a bucket of BLUEberries!

Blueberries sure are yummy in the tummy to eat,
but squish 'em and squirt 'em and blue berries forever
leave a blue stain
on whatever & wherever their splash splurts onto for sure.

So maybe that's how Gabriel's blue giraffe got his
beautiful blue.

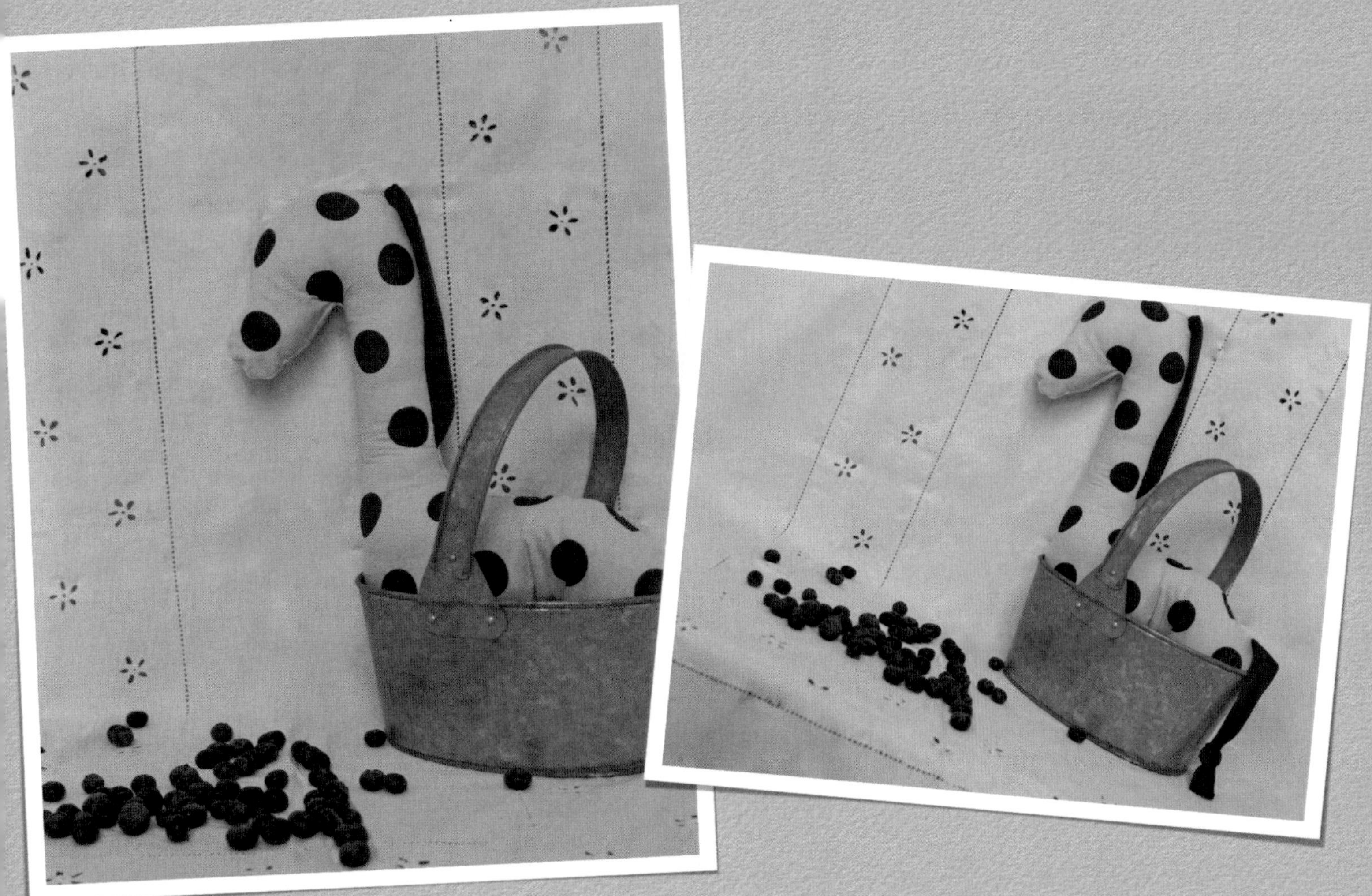

Maybe he got squirted by a squished blueberry splash that permanently stained him forever the color blue.

perhaps...

Perhaps Gabriel's blue giraffe

became blue when he flew so fast
he flew way up high into the sky to try to catch a cloud,
but instead of catching a cloud,
perhaps Gabriel's blue giraffe caught a draft
that made him so cold
he shivered & quivered
and
just flat out, plain old, turned burr chilly cold!

maybe...

you might wanna write & tell on this page
about how you imagine
Gabriel's giraffe might'a became blue?

perhaps...

if you wanna, you could create & draw on this page
a scene of how you think it could'a happened
& what it might'a could'a possibly looked like when Gabriel's giraffe became blue in the first place?

Ever wonder about those brown spots?
Why does Gabriel's blue giraffe have brown spots?
How do you suppose he might'a could'a gotten 'em?

Gabriel's blue giraffe
didn't by any chance
get KuRsPLatTurRed
by a
hail storm of
raining
plopping slopping
pouring down
chocolate chips that
melted onto him did he?

Semi-Sweet
CHOCOLATE
CHIPS
NET WT. 12 OZ (340g)

maybe...

Maybe it is possible to imagine that
Gabriel's blue giraffe got his giraffey brown spots

because he might'a liked to play Frisbee with
brown velcro Frisbees

because those kind of Frisbees could'a been much easier
to catch you know, or at least maybe we can
possibly imagine so.

perhaps...

Perhaps Gabriel's blue giraffe got his brown spots because
perhaps he once was chasing after a safari jeep
that drove through a chocolate milk mud puddle and
m a y b e   p e r h a p s
it's possible that the sPlaSh from the
chocolate milk mud puddle
StUck onto Gabriel's blue giraffe
on precisely all the spots
that are still StUck on the blue parts of Gabriel's blue
giraffe.

If that was in fact the Imaginable Mystery Explaining how
Gabriel's blue giraffe
got his brown spots,
well it just makes sense & must have been what
m a y b e   p e r h a p s
might'a could'a really happened,
because splashes of chocolate CaN leave brown spots on
blue giraffes you know,
or at least we can creatively imagine it to possibly be so.

Before and After pictures of Gabriel's Blue Giraffe
with and without
brown spots.

maybe...

you might write & tell on this page

how you imagine

Gabriel's blue giraffe possibly might'a gotten his brown spots?

perhaps...

you could create & draw on this page
a scene of how you think it could'a happened
& what it maybe perhaps possibly might'a could'a looked like
when Gabriel's giraffe first got his brown spots!

~no "the end" ~

M a y b e, p e r h a p s this is NOT t h e e n d.

I mean, how could you might possibly be sure
it ends here?!?

Truly creative imagination fun should always be
the kind of stuff that inspires us
to go on and on and create more and more
never ending fun....at least thats how my imagination works....hmmm....that
makes me wonder, "How did Zoe's zebra ever get her zany black
stripes....?????????????"

Made in the USA
Monee, IL
26 April 2024